WASHINGTON TEST PREP

Common Core Math

SBAC Mathematics

Grade 4

ISBN 978-1502969040

CONTENTS

INTRODUCTION
For Parents, Teachers, and Tutors

About the Common Core State Standards

The state of Washington has adopted the Common Core State Standards. These standards describe the skills that students are expected to have. Student learning throughout the year is based on these standards, and all the questions on the state tests assess these standards. Just like the real state tests, the questions in this book assess whether students have the knowledge and skills described in the Common Core State Standards.

About the Smarter Balanced Assessments

In the 2014-2015 school year, the state of Washington introduced new assessments. These are the Smarter Balanced, or the SBAC, assessments. This book contains ten practice sets that will help prepare students for the Smarter Balanced assessments. The practice sets cover all the Common Core skills assessed and provide practice with the types of questions and tasks found on the real assessments.

Types of Questions on the Smarter Balanced Assessments

The Smarter Balanced Assessments are taken online and include a wider range of question formats than previous tests. The question types found on the test are summarized below.

- Selected-response (single answer) - students select the one correct answer from four possible options.
- Selected-response (multiple answers) - students select one or more correct answers.
- Constructed-response - students provide a numerical or a text answer. These tasks may involve providing a simple numerical answer, filling in a blank, completing a missing number in an expression, completing numbers in a table, or writing either a simple text answer or a more advanced text answer that explains a mathematical concept or explains mathematical thinking.
- Technology-enhanced - students use online features to complete a task. These tasks may involve sorting items into groups, placing items in order, using fraction models, drawing shapes, plotting points on a number line or grid, or completing graphs and charts.
- Performance tasks - these are extended tasks that are completed in combination with a classroom activity and involve completing a number of related questions. The question formats are the same as those above. While the performance tasks are not the focus of this book, gaining experience with all the question types will help prepare students for the tasks.

This book contains a wide range of question types, including questions that mimic the formats that use online features. By completing the practice sets, students will develop all the Common Core skills they need and become familiar with all the question types they will encounter on the real Smarter Balanced assessments.

Taking the Tests

The first two practice sets introduce students to the assessments with 10 questions that cover all the common question types. These short tests will allow students to become familiar with Smarter Balanced questions before moving on to longer tests. These shorter tests may also be used as guided instruction before allowing students to complete the assessments on their own. The remaining practice sets each have 20 questions. Students will have an experience similar to the real assessments, but with fewer questions and a shorter test length. By completing the practice sets, students will have ongoing practice with assessment items, develop the Common Core math skills they need, gain experience with all types of test questions, and become comfortable with the Smarter Balanced assessments.

Common Core Math

Grade 4

Practice Set 1

Instructions

Read each question carefully. For each multiple-choice question, fill in the circle for the correct answer. For other types of questions, follow the directions given in the question.

You may use a ruler and a protractor to help you answer questions. You may not use a calculator on this test.

This test should take 45 minutes to complete.

---

1   The shaded models below represent two fractions.

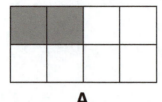 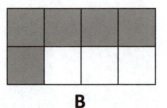

        A   **B**

How much greater is fraction B than fraction A?

Ⓐ $\dfrac{5}{8}$

Ⓑ $\dfrac{3}{8}$ ✓

Ⓒ $\dfrac{1}{3}$

Ⓓ $\dfrac{2}{5}$

2   Select **all** the calculations that are equal to 1.

☑ $\dfrac{1}{4} + \dfrac{1}{4} + \dfrac{1}{4} + \dfrac{1}{4}$

☐ $\dfrac{1}{2} + \dfrac{1}{2} + \dfrac{1}{4}$

☑ $\dfrac{1}{4} + \dfrac{3}{4}$

☑ $\dfrac{1}{2} + \dfrac{1}{4} + \dfrac{1}{4}$

☐ $\dfrac{2}{2} + \dfrac{2}{2}$

3   Brian checked in his bag at the airport. His bag weighed just over 21.9 kilograms. Which of the following could have been the weight of Brian's bag?

   Ⓐ   20.9 kg

   Ⓑ   21.4 kg

   Ⓒ   21.0 kg

   Ⓓ   22.1 kg

4   Gina states that the number 95 is a prime number. Which statement best explains how you can tell that Gina is incorrect?

   Ⓐ   The number 95 can be evenly divided by 5.

   Ⓑ   The number 95 is a two-digit number.

   Ⓒ   The number 95 is an odd number.

   Ⓓ   The number 95 is less than 100.

5   Select **all** the statements that are true.

   ☐   48.06 < 47.65

   ☐   32.55 < 32.09

   ☑   27.09 < 27.16

   ☐   11.88 < 11.73

   ☑   10.19 < 10.29

(6) Complete the missing numbers for each section of the area model below. Then use the area model to find the value of 42 × 28. Write your answer below.

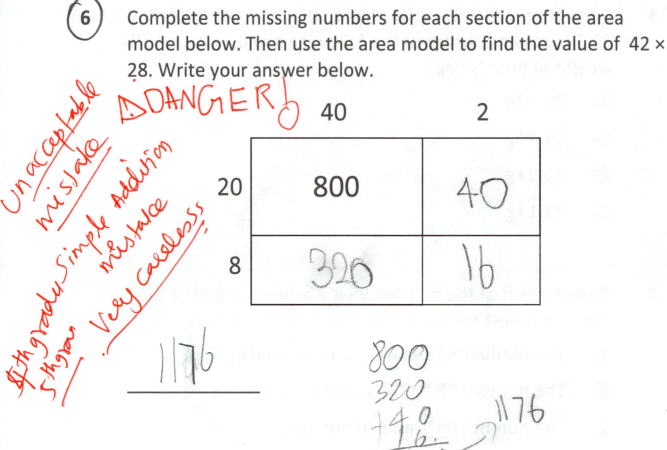

DANGER!

Unacceptable mistake

4th grade: Simple Addition mistake

5th grade: Very careless!

	40	2
20	800	40
8	320	16

1176

800
320
+16
———   → 1176

7   A pattern is made using the rules below.

• Start with the number 6.
• Add 8 to each term.

Complete the table to show the first five terms of the pattern.

Term	First	Second	Third	Fourth	Fifth
Number	6	14	22	30	38

✓

8 Priya measures the lengths of pieces of timber, in inches. The lengths measured are listed below.

$$2\frac{1}{4},\ 2\frac{3}{4},\ 2\frac{1}{2},\ 2\frac{1}{2},\ 2\frac{1}{4},\ 2,\ 2\frac{1}{4},\ 2\frac{1}{2},\ 2\frac{1}{4},\ 2\frac{3}{4}$$

a. Use the data to complete the line plot below.

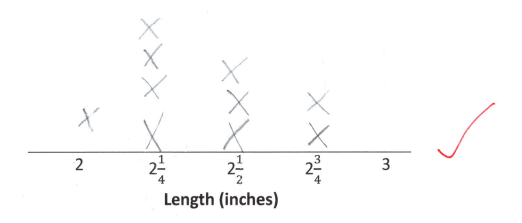

Pieces of Timber

Length (inches)

b. Priya uses all the timber pieces with the most common length. What is the total length of the pieces Priya uses? Write your answer below.

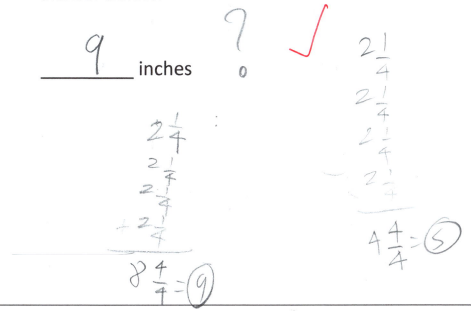

_____9_____ inches

9 Shade the diagram below to show the sum of $\frac{2}{4} + \frac{2}{4} + \frac{2}{4}$.

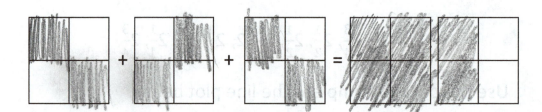

What is the sum of $\frac{2}{4} + \frac{2}{4} + \frac{2}{4}$? Write your answer as an improper fraction and a mixed number in lowest terms.

Improper fraction: $\frac{6}{4}$

Mixed number: $1\frac{1}{2}$

10 Rima is saving to buy a CD that costs $12. The money she has saved so far is shown below.

5¢   1¢   10¢   10¢

25¢

5¢   1¢   10¢

(3×10)=30
(5×2)=10
(25×1)=25
1×2¢ = 2

6 7¢
+
5 dollars

$5.67

How much money has Rima saved? Write your answer below.

$5.67 ✓

How much more money does Rima need to save to reach her goal of $12? Write your answer below.

$6.33

Subtraction
Addition
Mistake

END OF PRACTICE SET

Common Core Math

Grade 4

Practice Set 2

Instructions

Read each question carefully. For each multiple-choice question, fill in the circle for the correct answer. For other types of questions, follow the directions given in the question.

You may use a ruler and a protractor to help you answer questions. You may not use a calculator on this test.

This test should take 45 minutes to complete.

↗ typo: Circle

1   Greg divides a triangle into three equal sections, as shown below. What is the measure of angle *x*?

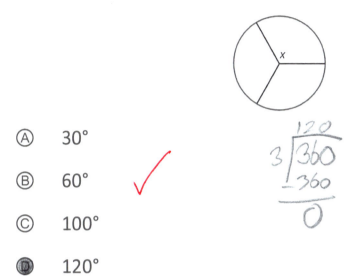

   Ⓐ   30°

   Ⓑ   60°   ✓

   Ⓒ   100°

   Ⓓ   120°

2   Select **all** the sums that have a value less than 1.

☑ $\frac{1}{3}+\frac{1}{3}$

☑ $\frac{1}{2}+\frac{1}{4}$

☐ $\frac{3}{4}+\frac{3}{4}$

☑ $\frac{3}{8}+\frac{3}{8}$ ✓

☑ $\frac{3}{5}+\frac{1}{5}$

☐ $\frac{5}{8}+\frac{7}{8}$

3   Look at the triangles below.

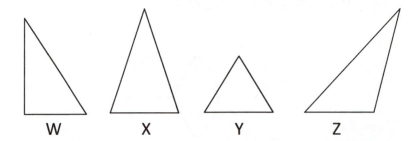

W   X   Y   Z

Connor classifies triangles X and Y as isosceles triangles because they have a pair of equal sides. What error has Connor made?

- Ⓐ   He has not recognized that triangle Y has more than 2 equal sides.

- Ⓑ   He has not considered the angle measures of triangle X.

- Ⓒ   He has not recognized that triangle X only has 2 equal sides.

- Ⓓ   He has not considered whether triangles X and Y have right angles.

4   Lawson wants to buy a camera that costs $120. He earns $8 per week by doing chores. If Lawson saves all his money, how many weeks will it take him to save $120?

- Ⓐ   12 weeks

- Ⓑ   15 weeks

- Ⓒ   18 weeks

- Ⓓ   20 weeks

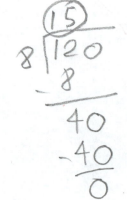

5 The table below lists the lengths of pieces of fabric in feet and yards.

Length in Feet	Length in Yards
6	2
12	4
15	5
30	10

Teresa wants a piece of fabric that is 9 yards long. What is the length of the piece of fabric in feet?

Ⓐ   3 ft

Ⓑ   13 ft

Ⓒ   27 ft

Ⓓ   90 ft

3 ft = 1 yd

9 × 3 = 27

6 Mia is setting up tables for a party. Each table can seat 6 people. Mia needs to seat 130 people. How many whole tables will Mia need to seat all 130 people? Write your answer below.

_____*22*_____ tables

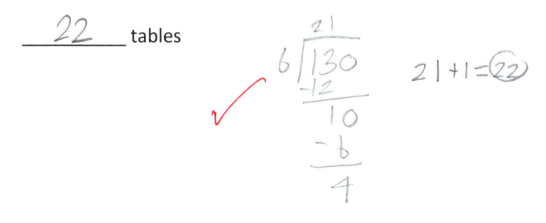

21 + 1 = 22

7   The angle below is a straight angle. Draw three lines to divide the angle into four equal angles.

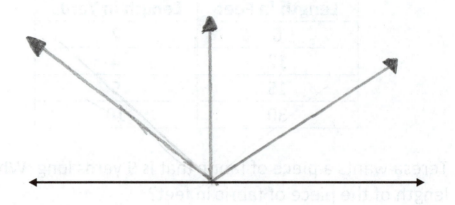

What is the measure of each smaller angle? Write your answer below.

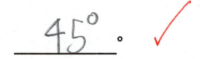

$45°$. ✓ °

What type of angle is each smaller angle? Circle the correct answer.

straight   (acute)   right   obtuse

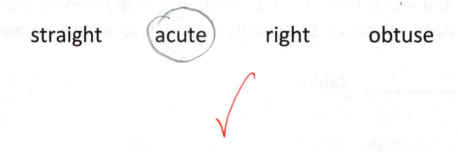

✓

8   The students in fourth grade held a vote on where to go for a field trip. The results are shown below.

Location	Number of Votes
Museum	16
Cinema	24
Zoo	36
Town Hall	12

Use the data in the table to complete the picture graph below.

Student Votes for Field Trip Location

Museum	✓✓✓✓
Cinema	✓✓✓✓ ✓✓
Zoo	✓✓✓✓✓✓✓✓✗
Town Hall	✓✓✓

✓ = 4 votes

Which two locations had the same number of votes in total as the zoo had? Write your answer below.

Cinema, Town Hall.

9   Samantha cut a piece of paper into smaller pieces that were each $\frac{1}{8}$ the size of the original piece of paper. Draw lines on the rectangles below to show **two** ways Samantha could have divided the paper.

Does every piece of paper cut have the same area even if they are not all the same shape? Explain how you can tell without finding the area of each piece.

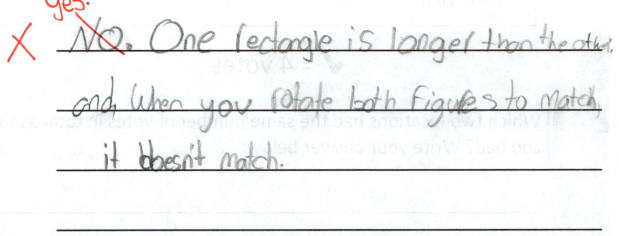

yes.

NO. One rectangle is longer than the other, and when you rotate both figures to match, it doesn't match.

10 Stan is putting a paved walkway in his front yard. He drew the plan below. On the diagram below, write the numbers in the boxes to show the missing dimensions.

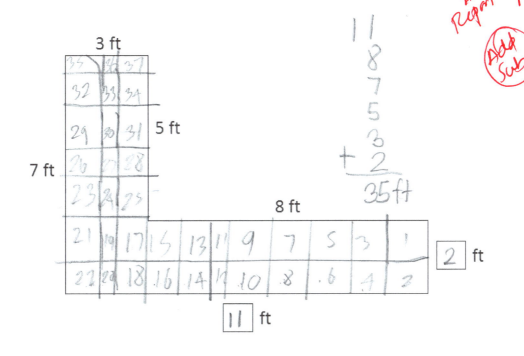

Find the perimeter of the walkway. Write your answer below.

_____ 35 X feet

Stan is using tiles that are 1 square foot each. How many tiles will he need to make the walkway? Write your answer below.

_____ 37 tiles

END OF PRACTICE SET

Common Core Math

Grade 4

Practice Set 3

Instructions

Read each question carefully. For each multiple-choice question, fill in the circle for the correct answer. For other types of questions, follow the directions given in the question.

You may use a ruler and a protractor to help you answer questions. You may not use a calculator on this test.

This test should take 60 minutes to complete.

---

1   Look at the letters below. Circle **all** the letters that have a line of symmetry.

A C F J P R T W Z

2   What kind of angle is each internal angle of the shape below?

Ⓐ   Acute

🅑   Right

Ⓒ   Obtuse

Ⓓ   Straight

3   Donna bought a lollipop for $0.60 and a candy for $0.15. How much change would Donna receive from $1?

Ⓐ $0.15

🅑 $0.25

Ⓒ $0.35

Ⓓ $0.75

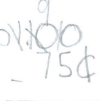

4 Sandra started walking to school at 8:45 a.m. It took her 25 minutes to get to school. What time did she get to school?

Ⓐ 9:00 a.m.

Ⓑ 9:10 a.m.

Ⓒ 9:15 a.m.

Ⓓ 9:20 a.m.

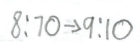

5 The table below shows the shirt number of six players on a basketball team.

Player	Shirt Number
Don	C 12
Jamie	P 17
Curtis	C 22
Chan	C 9
Wendell	P 31
Kevin	C 49

Determine whether each player's shirt number is prime or composite. Write P or C on the lines below to show your choice.

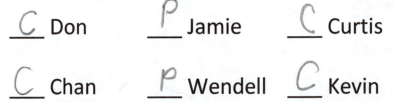

_C_ Don   _P_ Jamie   _C_ Curtis

_C_ Chan   _P_ Wendell   _C_ Kevin

6   Which shaded model represents $\frac{5}{4}$?

Ⓐ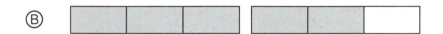

Ⓑ

Ⓒ

Ⓓ  ✓

7   The numbers below are arranged from least to greatest.

1,098   2,269   _____   2,350   2,699

least ←——————————————→ greatest

median

Which **two** numbers could go on the blank line?

☐   2,800

☐   2,401

☑   2,320

☐   2,185

☑   2,280   ✓

☐   2,239

8 Jenna buys 8 packets of letter paper. Each packet contains 12 sheets of paper. She uses 16 sheets of letter paper a week. How many weeks will it take her to use all the letter paper? Write your answer below.

_____ **6** _____ weeks

12×8

$16\overline{)96}$
$\underline{96}$
0

12
12
12
12
12
12
12
+12
96

32   2+
+32   2+
64   2+
132

9 Kenneth got on a train at 9:30 in the morning. He got off the train at 1:20 in the afternoon. How long was Kenneth on the train for? Write your answer below.

got it

_____ **4** _____ hours _____ **50** _____ minutes

on train
9:30Am

1:20PM
off train

10:00 +30min
11:00
12:00 4hr 50min
1:00
+20min

10 A fish tank can hold 20 liters of water. How many milliliters of water can the fish tank hold? Write your answer below.

_____ **20,000** _____ ml

1,000ml = 1L

20×1,000
=20,000

11 The table below shows the number of meals a café served on four different days.

Monday	Tuesday	Wednesday	Thursday
1,487	1,510	1,461	1,469

Place the numbers in order from the least to the most number of meals served.

$\underline{1,461}$ < $\underline{1,469}$ < $\underline{1,487}$ < $\underline{1,510}$
least   Some   many   Greatest

On Friday, the café served 200 more meals than on Tuesday. How many meals did the café serve on Friday? Write your answer below.

$\underline{1,710}$

1,510
+ 200
⎯⎯⎯
(1,710)

Time problem
pay attention

5:45
28
⎯⎯
5:70
6:10

5:(45) + 28 mins
6:10.

12 The table below shows the number of male and female students at Hill Street School.

Gender	Number
Male	2,629
Female	2,518

How many students go to the school in all? Write your answer below.

$$\begin{array}{r} {}^{1}2\,{}^{1}629 \\ +\ 2518 \\ \hline 5,147 \end{array}$$

How many more male students are there than female students? Write your answer below.

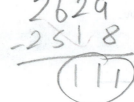

$$\begin{array}{r} 2629 \\ -2518 \\ \hline 111 \end{array}$$

13 A right triangle is shown below.

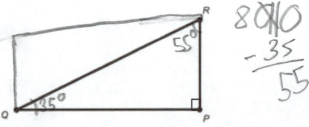

$$\begin{array}{r} 8\,0\!\!\!/\,0 \\ -\ 35 \\ \hline 55 \end{array}$$

If angle *Q* measures 35°, what is the measure of angle *R*? Write your answer below.

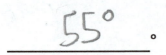

55° °

14 The top of Kevin's dining room table is 4 feet long and 3 feet wide. Kevin wants to cover the middle of the table with tiles. He plans to leave a 6 inch border around the edge of the table and tile the center. Shade the area he will cover on the diagram below.

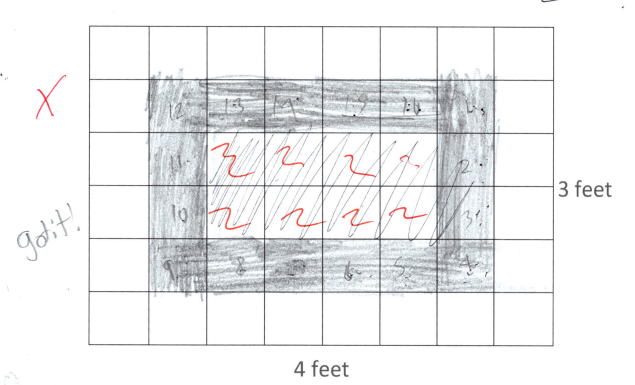

3 feet

4 feet

How many square feet of tiles will he need? Write your answer below.

_____ square feet

15 What value of *n* makes each number sentence below true? Write each value below.

35 + 3 = *n* + 5   *n* = ___33___ ✓

80 − 24 = 90 − *n*   *n* = ___34___ ✓

20 + 20 = 2*n*   *n* = ___20___ ✓

100 − 37 = *n* − 17   *n* = ___63___

16 Megan arranged some beads in the pattern shown below. Draw the correct two beads that continue the pattern below.

17 Which shaded model shows a fraction greater than $\frac{4}{5}$?

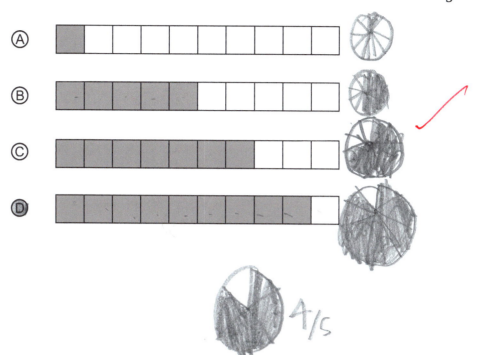

Ⓐ

Ⓑ

Ⓒ

Ⓓ

4/5

18 What is the number 457,869 rounded to the nearest ten thousand and the nearest thousand? Write your answers below.

Nearest ten thousand: _460,000_

Nearest thousand: _458,000_

19 Which is the best estimate of the length of a football?

   Ⓐ   10 inches

   Ⓑ   10 millimeters ✓ ⟨17/20⟩

   Ⓒ   10 meters

   Ⓓ   10 yards

20 Mia bought a milkshake. She was given the change shown below. How much change was Mia given? Write your answer below.

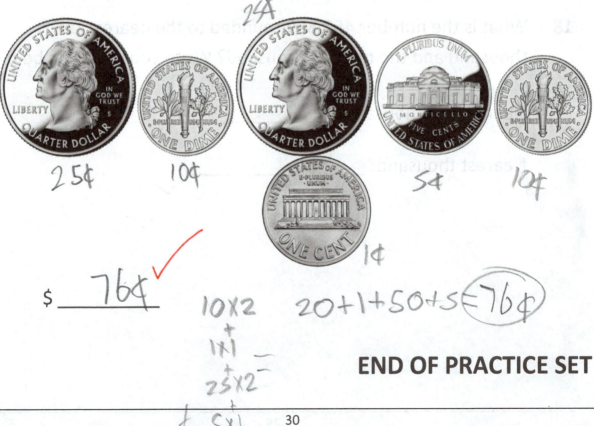

25¢   10¢   24¢   5¢   10¢

1¢

$ ___76¢___ ✓

10×2
+
1×1
=
25×2
+
5×1

20+1+50+5=⟨76¢⟩

END OF PRACTICE SET

Common Core Math

Grade 4

Practice Set 4

Instructions

Read each question carefully. For each multiple-choice question, fill in the circle for the correct answer. For other types of questions, follow the directions given in the question.

You may use a ruler and a protractor to help you answer questions. You may not use a calculator on this test.

This test should take 60 minutes to complete.

1   Which measurement is the best estimate of the length of a swimming pool?

ⓐ   10 millimeters

ⓑ   10 centimeters

ⓒ   10 kilometers

ⓓ   10 meters

2   Circle **all** the angles of the shapes below that are obtuse.

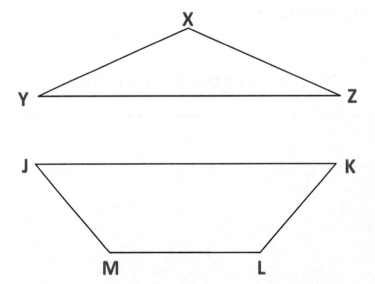

3 What part of the model is shaded?

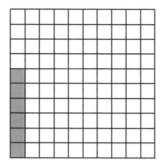

Ⓐ   6.0

Ⓑ   0.6

Ⓒ   0.06

Ⓓ   0.006

4 Which value of *p* makes the equation below true?

$$p \div 7 = 9$$

Ⓐ   49

Ⓑ   56

Ⓒ   63

Ⓓ   81

5   Shade the **two** diagrams below to represent fractions equivalent to $\frac{1}{2}$.

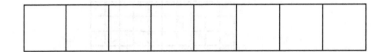

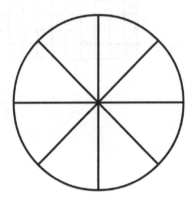

6   What is the rule to find the value of a term in the sequence below?

Position, *n*	Value of Term
1	3
2	6
3	9
4	12

Ⓐ $n \times 2$

Ⓑ $n \times 3$

Ⓒ $n + 2$

Ⓓ $n + 3$

7   Which statements are true? Select **all** the correct statements.

☐   386 > 389

☐   412 > 450

☐   589 < 596

☐   611 < 610

☐   805 > 799

☐   465 > 481

☐   987 < 937

☐   152 < 170

8   What is the sum of $\frac{1}{10}$ and $\frac{3}{100}$? Write your answer below.

_____

9   Mrs. Smyth has 82 colored pencils. She wants to divide them evenly between 8 people. How many whole pencils will each person receive? Write your answer below.

_____ pencils

10   The table below shows the number of students in each grade at the David Hall School.

Grade	Number of Students
3	254
4	235
5	229

How many students are there in all? Write your answer below.

_____ students

11 The diagram below represents the sum of $\frac{1}{4}$, $\frac{1}{4}$, and $\frac{1}{4}$. Shade the last grid to show the sum of $\frac{1}{4}$, $\frac{1}{4}$, and $\frac{1}{4}$.

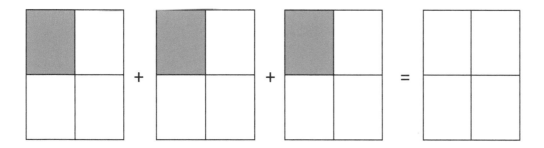

What is the sum of $\frac{1}{4}$, $\frac{1}{4}$, and $\frac{1}{4}$? Write your answer below.

_____

On the lines below, explain how the diagram helped you find the sum.

_____

_____

_____

_____

_____

12 What is the area of the square shown below? Write your answer below. Be sure to include the correct units.

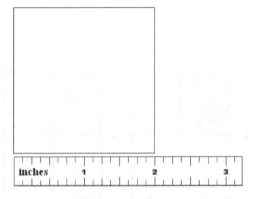

Area: _____

13 Jeremy had the coins shown below.

He swapped all the coins for nickels of the same total value. How many nickels should he have received? Write your answer below.

_____ nickels

14   A trapezoid is shown below. Circle **all** the acute angles of the trapezoid below.

On the lines below, explain how you can determine whether the angles are acute without measuring them.

_____

_____

_____

_____

_____

15   The fine for having a DVD overdue is a basic fee of $4 plus an additional $2 for each day that the movie is overdue.

Complete the equation below to show c, the amount of the fine in dollars when a DVD is overdue for d days.

$$c = \underline{\hspace{1cm}} d + \underline{\hspace{1cm}}$$

Use the equation to find the cost of the fine when a DVD is overdue for 6 days. Write your answer below.

$\underline{\hspace{3cm}}$

16 The table below shows the total number of pieces of bread Aaron used to make peanut butter and jelly sandwiches.

Number of Sandwiches	Number of Pieces of Bread
2	6
4	12
8	24

Complete the missing number to show the relationship between the number of sandwiches and the number of pieces of bread.

Sandwiches × ⬜ = pieces of bread

17 Which unit would be best to use to measure the length of a box of tissues?

Ⓐ   Yards

Ⓑ   Miles

Ⓒ   Centimeters

Ⓓ   Kilometers

18 Which **two** numbers are multiples of 8? Select the **two** correct answers.

☐ 2

☐ 4

☐ 18

☐ 32

☐ 36

☐ 56

19 What is the sum of $1\frac{3}{4}$ and $\frac{1}{2}$? Complete the diagram below to help you find the answer.

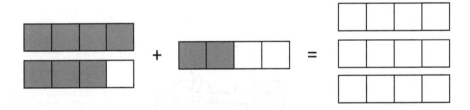

Ⓐ 2

Ⓑ $2\frac{1}{4}$

Ⓒ $2\frac{1}{2}$

Ⓓ $2\frac{3}{4}$

20 Joseph earns $8 per hour. In one week, he earned $280. How many hours did Joseph work that week? Write your answer below.

_____ hours

Joseph wants to earn $360 each week. How many hours will Joseph have to work to earn $360? Write your answer below.

_____ hours

Joseph decides to ask for a pay rise to $9 per hour. How many hours will Joseph have to work to earn $360 at $9 per hour? Write your answer below.

_____ hours

Joseph gets his pay rise to $9 per hour and works 30 hours. How much would Joseph make that week? Write your answer below.

$ _____

END OF PRACTICE SET

Common Core Math

Grade 4

Practice Set 5

Instructions

Read each question carefully. For each multiple-choice question, fill in the circle for the correct answer. For other types of questions, follow the directions given in the question.

You may use a ruler and a protractor to help you answer questions. You may not use a calculator on this test.

This test should take 60 minutes to complete.

---

1   What is the perimeter and area of the rectangle? Write your answers below.

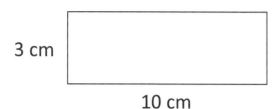

3 cm

10 cm

Perimeter: _____

Area: _____

2   An array for the number 36 is shown below.

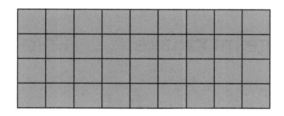

Which numbers are factors of 36? Select **all** the correct answers.

☐   4

☐   5

☐   7

☐   8

☐   9

3 The table below shows the cost of food at a diner.

Drinks		Meals	
Small milkshake	$1.80	Plain hamburger	$3.50
Large milkshake	$2.00	Chicken burger	$4.20
Small soda	$1.10	Hotdog	$2.60
Large soda	$1.50	Meatball sub	$3.10
Fruit juice	$1.90	Quiche	$2.10

Lisa bought two different items and spent exactly $4.00. Circle the **two** items that Lisa bought.

Small milkshake   Plain hamburger

Large milkshake   Chicken burger

Small soda   Hotdog

Large soda   Meatball sub

Fruit juice   Quiche

4   The table below shows the entry cost for a museum.

Adult	$10 per person
Child	$8 per person
Family (2 adults and 2 children)	$30 per family

How much would a family of 2 adults and 2 children save by buying a family ticket instead of individual tickets?

Ⓐ $2

Ⓑ $6

Ⓒ $8

Ⓓ $10

5   Maria is reading a book with 286 pages. She has read 38 pages. To the nearest ten, how many pages does Maria have left to read?

Ⓐ   240

Ⓑ   250

Ⓒ   260

Ⓓ   270

6 A box of beads contains 240 beads. Chang buys 4 boxes of beads. How many beads did Chang buy? Write your answer below.

_____ beads

7 Liam has 6 pots he grows herbs in. He planted mint in $\frac{1}{4}$ of each pot. What fraction of a pot is the mint in total?

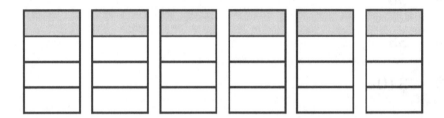

Ⓐ $1\frac{1}{2}$ pots

Ⓑ $1\frac{1}{4}$ pots

Ⓒ $1\frac{1}{6}$ pots

Ⓓ $1\frac{1}{8}$ pots

8 What is the measure of the angle shown below? Write your answer below.

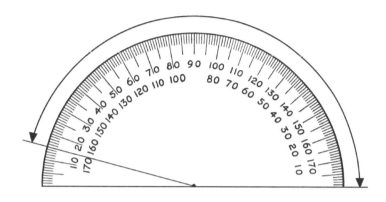

_____°

9 A pet shop sells fish for $3 each. The pet shop sold $96 worth of fish one day. How many fish did the pet shop sell that day?

Ⓐ 32

Ⓑ 36

Ⓒ 48

Ⓓ 288

10 Which number is a factor of 57?

Ⓐ 11

Ⓑ 13

Ⓒ 17

Ⓓ 19

11 Which numbers are multiples of 6? Circle **all** the correct numbers.

2	3	12	20
24	30	44	46
50	54	66	70

12 A motorbike has a weight of 255 kilograms. What is the weight of the motorbike in grams? Write your answer below.

_____ grams

13 The fraction $\frac{56}{100}$ is plotted on the number line below. What decimal is plotted on the number line?

(A)   5.6

(B)   5.06

(C)   0.56

(D)   0.506

14 The table shows the relationship between feet and inches. Complete the table by showing how many feet would have a value of 72 inches.

Feet	Inches
1	12
2	24
3	36
	72

15 The angle that is formed between two lines has a measure of 95°. Which term describes this angle?

Ⓐ   Acute

Ⓑ   Right

Ⓒ   Obtuse

Ⓓ   Straight

16 Jayden wants to find the length of a paperclip. Which unit would Jayden be best to use?

Ⓐ   Yards

Ⓑ   Feet

Ⓒ   Kilometers

Ⓓ   Centimeters

17 There are 1,920 students at Jenna's school. Which of these is another way to write 1,920?

Ⓐ   1,000 + 900 + 20

Ⓑ   1,000 + 900 + 2

Ⓒ   1,000 + 90 + 20

Ⓓ   1,000 + 90 + 2

18 Which of the following describes the rule for this pattern?

1, 3, 6, 8, 11, 13, 16

Ⓐ   Add 2, add 3

Ⓑ   Add 2, multiply by 2

Ⓒ   Multiply by 3, multiply by 2

Ⓓ   Multiply by 3, add 3

19 Troy swapped 2 quarters for coins with the same value. Which of these could Troy have swapped his 2 quarters for? Select **all** the correct answers.

☐   25 pennies

☐   20 nickels

☐   10 nickels

☐   10 dimes

☐   4 nickels and 4 dimes

☐   4 dimes and 10 pennies

20 Which number goes in the box to make the equation below true? Write your answer in the box below.

$$54 \div \boxed{} = 9$$

END OF PRACTICE SET

Common Core Math

Grade 4

Practice Set 6

Instructions

Read each question carefully. For each multiple-choice question, fill in the circle for the correct answer. For other types of questions, follow the directions given in the question.

You may use a ruler and a protractor to help you answer questions. You may not use a calculator on this test.

This test should take 60 minutes to complete.

1 A pumpkin weighs 4 pounds. How many ounces does the pumpkin weigh?

Ⓐ   32 ounces

Ⓑ   40 ounces

Ⓒ   48 ounces

Ⓓ   64 ounces

2 The table below shows the population of 3 towns.

Town	Population
Franklin	18,725
Torine	24,214
Maxville	16,722

Which number sentence shows the best way to estimate how much greater the population of Torine is than Franklin?

Ⓐ   24,000 − 16,000 = 8,000

Ⓑ   24,000 − 17,000 = 7,000

Ⓒ   24,000 − 18,000 = 6,000

Ⓓ   24,000 − 19,000 = 5,000

3   A movie made $5,256,374 in its first weekend. What does the 2 in this number represent?

Ⓐ   Two thousand

Ⓑ   Twenty thousand

Ⓒ   Two hundred thousand

Ⓓ   Two million

4   Select **all** the shapes that have at least one line of symmetry.

☐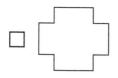

☐

☐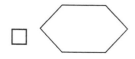

☐

☐

5   The table shows the amount Davis spent on phone calls each month.

Month	Amount
April	$9.22
May	$9.09
June	$9.18
July	$9.05

In which month did Davis spend the least on phone calls? Write your answer below.

_____

In which month did Davis spend closest to $9.15 on phone calls? Write your answer below.

_____

In August, Davis spent $0.20 more than in July. How much did Davis spend in August? Write your answer below.

$ _____

6   Emma grouped some numbers into two groups, as shown below.

Group 1	Group 2
14	21
86	79
922	325
388	683

Circle all the numbers that should be placed in Group 2.

18   630   864   57

247   121   156   93

7   The sizes of the drill bits in a set are measured in inches. Which size drill bits are greater than $\frac{1}{2}$ inch? Select **all** the correct answers.

☐ $\frac{3}{8}$ inch

☐ $\frac{7}{16}$ inch

☐ $\frac{1}{8}$ inch

☐ $\frac{9}{16}$ inch

☐ $\frac{7}{12}$ inch

8   What is the rule to find the value of a term in the sequence below?

Position, n	Value of Term
1	3
2	4
3	5
4	6
5	7

Ⓐ $2n$

Ⓑ $3n$

Ⓒ $n + 2$

Ⓓ $n + 3$

9   A square garden has side lengths of 8 inches. What is the area of the garden? Write your answer below. Be sure to include the correct units.

_____

10 Look at the line segments shown below.

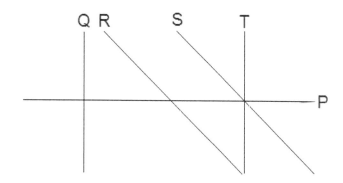

Which **two** pairs of line segments are parallel? Write your answers below.

Line segments _____ and _____

Line segments _____ and _____

11 Which of these is the best estimate of the length of a baseball bat?

Ⓐ   3 inches

Ⓑ   3 feet

Ⓒ   3 millimeters

Ⓓ   3 centimeters

12 There are 40,260 people watching a baseball game. Which of these is another way to write 40,260?

Ⓐ 4 + 2 + 6

Ⓑ 40 + 2 + 60

Ⓒ 40,000 + 200 + 6

Ⓓ 40,000 + 200 + 60

13 The model below is shaded to show $2\frac{4}{10}$.

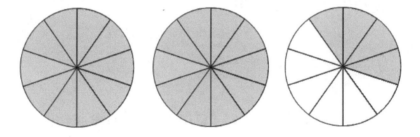

What decimal does the model represent? Write your answer below.

_____

14 Which of the following is another way to write the numeral 600,032?

Ⓐ   Six hundred thousand and thirty-two

Ⓑ   Six million and thirty-two

Ⓒ   Six hundred and thirty-two

Ⓓ   Six thousand and thirty-two

15 The drawing below shows a kite.

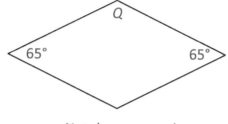

Not drawn to scale

What is the measure of angle Q?

Ⓐ   57.5°

Ⓑ   65°

Ⓒ   115°

Ⓓ   230°

16   Which numbers are composite numbers? Select **all** the correct answers.

☐   67

☐   73

☐   77

☐   81

☐   89

☐   91

17   What is 83,462 rounded to the nearest hundred and the nearest ten? Write your answers below.

Nearest hundred: _____

Nearest ten: _____

18 Which **two** pairs of numbers complete the equation below?

$$\boxed{} \times 100 = \boxed{}$$

☐ 60 and 600

☐ 60 and 6,000

☐ 60 and 60,000

☐ 6 and 60

☐ 6 and 600

☐ 6 and 6000

19 What is the measure of the angle shown below?

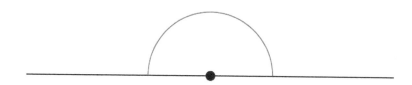

Ⓐ 45°

Ⓑ 90°

Ⓒ 100°

Ⓓ 180°

20 Kai found the coins shown below in the sofa.

What is the value of the coins that Kai found? Write your answer below.

$ _____

Kai gave 3 coins totaling 55 cents to his sister. Which three coins did Kai give to his sister? Write your answer below.

_____

After giving the coins to his sister, how much money would Kai have left? Write your answer below.

$ _____

END OF PRACTICE SET

Common Core Math

Grade 4

Practice Set 7

Instructions

Read each question carefully. For each multiple-choice question, fill in the circle for the correct answer. For other types of questions, follow the directions given in the question.

You may use a ruler and a protractor to help you answer questions. You may not use a calculator on this test.

This test should take 60 minutes to complete.

1 Which figure below does NOT have any parallel sides?

Ⓐ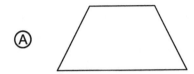

Ⓑ

Ⓒ

Ⓓ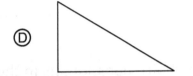

2 What is another way to write the fraction $\frac{9}{4}$?

Ⓐ $1\frac{1}{4}$

Ⓑ $1\frac{3}{4}$

Ⓒ $2\frac{1}{4}$

Ⓓ $2\frac{3}{4}$

3   Jackie made this table to show how much she received in tips on the four days that she worked. On which day did Jackie earn closest to $32?

Day	Amount
Monday	$32.55
Tuesday	$31.98
Thursday	$30.75
Friday	$32.09

Ⓐ   Monday

Ⓑ   Tuesday

Ⓒ   Thursday

Ⓓ   Friday

4   Bruce is counting his quarters. He puts them in 35 piles of 5. How could you work out the total value of the quarters?

Ⓐ   Divide 35 by 5, and multiply the result by $0.25

Ⓑ   Multiply 35 by 5, and multiply the result by $0.25

Ⓒ   Divide 35 by 5, and divide the result by $0.25

Ⓓ   Multiply 35 by 5, and divide the result by $0.25

5 A bakery makes muffins in batches of 12. The bakery made 18 batches of muffins. Which is the best estimate of the number of muffins made?

   Ⓐ   100

   Ⓑ   400

   Ⓒ   250

   Ⓓ   200

6 Katie saw the sign below at a fruit stand.

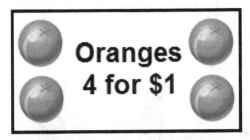

Oranges
4 for $1

If Katie spent $6 on oranges, how many oranges would she get? Write your answer on the line below.

_____

7   The normal price of a CD player is $298. During a sale, the CD player was $45 less than the normal price. What was the sale price of the CD player?

Ⓐ $343

Ⓑ $333

Ⓒ $263

Ⓓ $253

8   Complete each calculation below. Write the numbers on the lines.

$8 \times 9 =$ _____

$6 \times 6 =$ _____

$70 \times 4 =$ _____

$3 \times 111 =$ _____

9 Bagels are sold in packets of 4 or packets of 6. Kieran needs to buy exactly 32 bagels. Which set of packets could Kieran buy?

Ⓐ   2 packets of 4 bagels and 4 packets of 6 bagels

Ⓑ   3 packets of 4 bagels and 3 packets of 6 bagels

Ⓒ   4 packets of 4 bagels and 2 packets of 6 bagels

Ⓓ   5 packets of 4 bagels and 1 packet of 6 bagels

10 A bakery needs to order 60 eggs. There are 12 eggs in each carton. Which number sentence could be used to find c, the number of cartons the bakery should order?

Ⓐ $12 \times c = 60$

Ⓑ $12 \div c = 60$

Ⓒ $60 - 12 = c$

Ⓓ $60 \times 12 = c$

11 Which number has a 4 in the millions place?

   Ⓐ   8,340,386

   Ⓑ   5,468,950

   Ⓒ   4,082,663

   Ⓓ   8,934,159

12 Which figure below shows a line of symmetry?

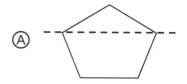

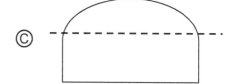

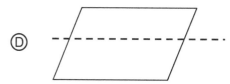

13   Plot the decimal 1.75 on the number line.

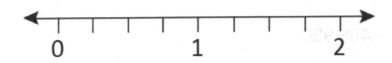

What fraction is equivalent to 1.75? Write your answer below.

_____

14   Shade the model to show $1\frac{7}{10}$.

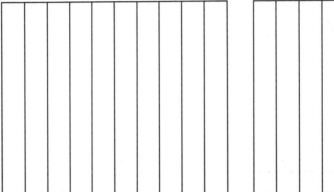 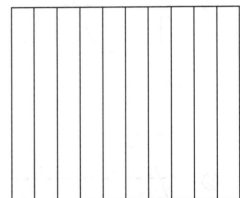

Write the mixed number $1\frac{7}{10}$ as an improper fraction. Write your answer below.

_____

15   Look at the number pattern below.

$$5, 11, 17, 23, 29, 35, \underline{\quad}$$

If the pattern continues, which number will come next? Write your answer below.

_____

Explain how you found your answer.

_____

_____

_____

Will all the numbers in the pattern be odd numbers? Explain your answer.

_____

_____

_____

16 Salma drew these shapes.

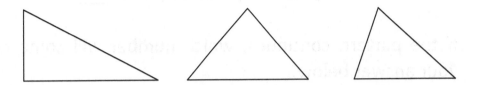

Identify the shape that has a line of symmetry. Draw the line of symmetry on the shape you identified.

On the lines below, describe how you can tell that the shape has a line of symmetry.

_____

_____

_____

_____

_____

17 Identify the place value for each digit in the number 234.15. Draw a line to match each digit with its place value.

1   hundreds

2   hundredths

3   ones

4   tens

5   tenths

Write the missing numbers on the lines to show 234.15 in expanded form.

$(\underline{} \times 100) + (\underline{} \times 10) + (\underline{} \times 1) + (\underline{} \times \frac{1}{10}) + (\underline{} \times \frac{1}{100})$

18   A school divided its grade 4 students into 6 classes. There were exactly 26 students in each class. How many students were there in all? Write your answer below.

_____ students

19   A park has a length of 60 feet and a width of 40 feet. What is the area of the park? Write your answer below.

_____ square feet

20   Sort the figures below by placing the correct letters in each column of the table.

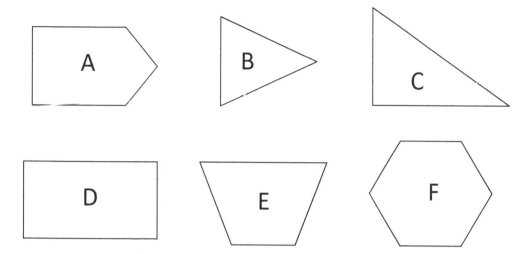

1 or more right angles	1 or more pairs of parallel sides	1 or more pairs of perpendicular sides

END OF PRACTICE SET

Common Core Math

Grade 4

Practice Set 8

Instructions

Read each question carefully. For each multiple-choice question, fill in the circle for the correct answer. For other types of questions, follow the directions given in the question.

You may use a ruler and a protractor to help you answer questions. You may not use a calculator on this test.

This test should take 60 minutes to complete.

---

1   Josephine boarded a train at 10:10 a.m. She got off the train at 12:55 p.m. How many minutes was she on the train for? Write your answer below.

_____ minutes

2   Ari is putting photos in an album. He can fit 6 photos on each page. He has 44 photos to place in the album. If he puts 6 photos on each page and the remainder on the last page, how many photos will be on the last page?

Ⓐ   1

Ⓑ   2

Ⓒ   3

Ⓓ   4

3   Which is a prime factor of the composite number 24?

Ⓐ   8

Ⓑ   7

Ⓒ   6

Ⓓ   3

4   Mia is setting up tables for a party. Each table can seat 6 people. Mia needs to seat 42 people. Mia wants to find how many tables she will need. Complete the equation below that shows how to find the number of tables she will need, t.

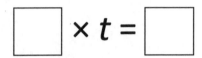

$$\boxed{} \times t = \boxed{}$$

5   Vienna bought a packet of 12 gift cards. She used 2 gift cards and her sister used 3 gift cards. What fraction of the gift cards did the two sisters use?

Ⓐ $\dfrac{1}{2}$

Ⓑ $\dfrac{2}{3}$

Ⓒ $\dfrac{5}{12}$

Ⓓ $\dfrac{1}{6}$

6   Zoe has 90 small lollipops, 30 large lollipops, and 55 candies. What is a common factor Zoe could use to divide the treats into equal groups? Circle the correct answer.

2   3   5   9   10   15

7 A school cafeteria offered four Italian meal choices. The table below shows the number of meals served of each type.

Meal	Number Served
Pasta	151
Pizza	167
Salad	213
Risotto	117

Which is the best estimate of the total number of meals served?

Ⓐ 630

Ⓑ 650

Ⓒ 660

Ⓓ 670

8 Jay made 8 trays of 6 muffins each. He gave 12 muffins away. Which expression can be used to find how many muffins he had left?

Ⓐ $(8 \times 6) - 12$

Ⓑ $(8 \times 6) + 12$

Ⓒ $8 + 6 - 12$

Ⓓ $8 + 6 + 12$

9   Stevie had $1.45. She bought a drink for $1.20. Stevie was given one coin as change. Which coin should Stevie have been given?

    Ⓐ   A dime

    Ⓑ   A penny

    Ⓒ   A quarter

    Ⓓ   A nickel

10   Which of these is the best estimate of the mass of a watermelon?

    Ⓐ   5 ounces

    Ⓑ   5 grams

    Ⓒ   5 pounds

    Ⓓ   5 milligrams

11   The factor tree for the number 60 is shown below.

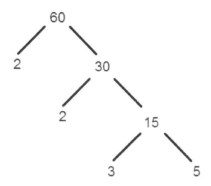

According to the factor tree, which statements are true? Select **all** the correct statements.

☐   The number 30 is a prime number.

☐   The number 60 is a composite number.

☐   The only prime factor of 60 is 2.

☐   The numbers 15 and 30 are prime factors of 60.

☐   The numbers 2, 3, and 5 are prime factors of 60.

☐   The numbers 4 and 6 are factors of 60.

12 Each number that was put into the number machine below changed according to a rule.

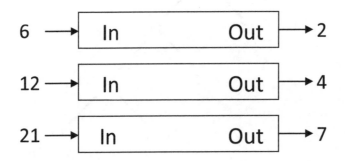

Complete the equation that describes the rule for the number machine. Add the correct symbol to the first box and the correct number to the second box.

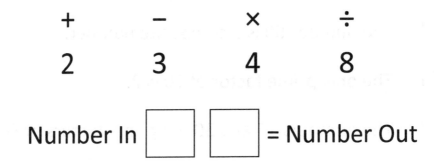

13 Which digit is in the thousands place in the number 6,124,853?

Ⓐ   6

Ⓑ   1

Ⓒ   2

Ⓓ   4

14 Malcolm surveyed some people to find out how many pets they owned. The line plot shows the results of the survey.

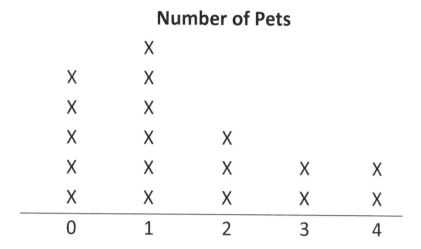

How many people owned 2 or more pets? Write your answer below.

_____ people

15 The shaded model below represents a fraction.

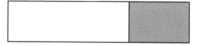

Shade the model below to represent an equivalent fraction.

16 What decimal does the shaded model below represent? Write your answer below.

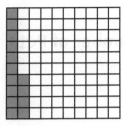

_____

17 The diagram shows two sets of black and white stickers.

Which of these compares the portion of black stickers in each set?

Ⓐ $\frac{8}{9} > \frac{2}{3}$

Ⓑ $\frac{8}{9} < \frac{2}{9}$

Ⓒ $\frac{2}{3} < \frac{1}{3}$

Ⓓ $\frac{1}{9} > \frac{6}{9}$

18 The grade 4 students at Diane's school are collecting cans for a food drive. The table below shows how many cans each class collected.

Class	Number of Cans
Miss Adams	36
Mr. Walsh	28
Mrs. Naroda	47

Which is the best way to estimate the number of cans collected in all?

Ⓐ   30 + 20 + 40 = ?

Ⓑ   30 + 30 + 40 = ?

Ⓒ   40 + 30 + 50 = ?

Ⓓ   40 + 30 + 40 = ?

19 Convert 12 quarts to pints and cups. Write your answers below.

12 quarts = _____ pints

12 quarts = _____ cups

20 Which of these could be two of the angle measures of the right triangle below?

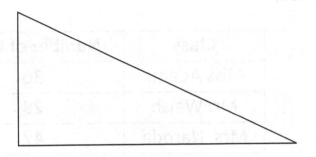

Ⓐ   20° and 60°

Ⓑ   25° and 65°

Ⓒ   30° and 70°

Ⓓ   45° and 75°

END OF PRACTICE SET

Common Core Math

Grade 4

Practice Set 9

Instructions

Read each question carefully. For each multiple-choice question, fill in the circle for the correct answer. For other types of questions, follow the directions given in the question.

You may use a ruler and a protractor to help you answer questions. You may not use a calculator on this test.

This test should take 60 minutes to complete.

1 If *n* is a number in the pattern, which rule can be used to find the next number in the pattern?

$$4, 6, 8, 10, 12, 14, 16, \ldots$$

Ⓐ $n + 2$

Ⓑ $n - 2$

Ⓒ $n + 4$

Ⓓ $n - 4$

2 What part of the model is shaded?

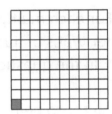

Ⓐ   0.01

Ⓑ   0.1

Ⓒ   1

Ⓓ   10

3   Which of these shapes has exactly one pair of perpendicular sides?

Ⓐ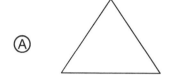

Ⓑ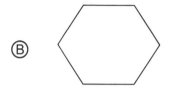

Ⓒ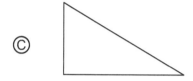

Ⓓ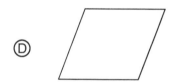

4   Draw a line on each shape below to show the line of symmetry.

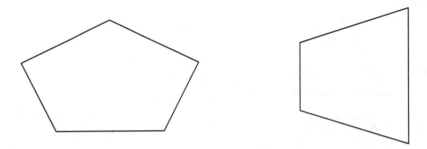

5   Thomas scored 5 times as many points in a basketball game as Jarrod. If Jarrod's number of points is represented as x, which of these shows Thomas's number of points?

Ⓐ $5 + x$

Ⓑ $5 - x$

Ⓒ $\dfrac{5}{x}$

Ⓓ $5x$

6   Which of the following is a right triangle?

Ⓐ

Ⓑ

Ⓒ

Ⓓ

7   Madison used $1\frac{3}{4}$ cups of milk to make a milkshake. Which of the following is another way to write $1\frac{3}{4}$?

Ⓐ $\frac{1}{4} + \frac{3}{4}$

Ⓑ $\frac{4}{4} + \frac{3}{4}$

Ⓒ $\frac{1 \times 3}{4}$

Ⓓ $\frac{4 \times 3}{4}$

8   Andy was buying a used car. He had four cars in his price range to choose from. The four cars had the odometer readings listed below.

Car	Toyota	Ford	Honda	Saturn
Reading (miles)	22,482	21,987	23,689	22,501

Place the cars in order from the lowest reading to the highest reading. Write the names of the cars below.

Lowest   _____

_____

_____

Highest   _____

9   Which number goes in the box to make the equation below true? Write your answer in the box below.

$$44 \div \boxed{} = 11$$

10 Which of the following has a mass of about 1 gram?

  Ⓐ   A dictionary

  Ⓑ   A pen

  Ⓒ   A car

  Ⓓ   A paper clip

11 Shade the models below to show two fractions equivalent to $\frac{6}{10}$. Then write the two fractions shaded on the lines below.

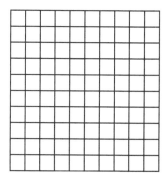

Fractions: _____ and _____

12 Jade made a pattern using marbles. The first four steps of the pattern are shown below.

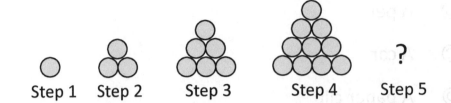

If Jade continues the pattern, how many marbles will she need for Step 5? Write your answer below.

_____

13 A bookstore sold 40,905 books in May. Which of these is another way to write 40,905?

Ⓐ   Four thousand nine hundred and five

Ⓑ   Forty thousand ninety five

Ⓒ   Four thousand ninety five

Ⓓ   Forty thousand nine hundred and five

14 The thermometers below show the air temperature at 10 a.m. and 2 p.m. one day.

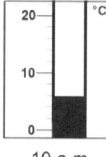

10 a.m.

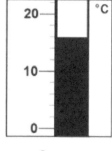

2 p.m.

How much did the temperature rise by from 10 a.m. to 2 p.m.?

Ⓐ   5°C

Ⓑ   6°C

Ⓒ   10°C

Ⓓ   16°C

15 Which **two** pairs of numbers correctly complete this table? Select the **two** correct answers.

Number	Number × 10
850	8,500
3,501	35,010
19	190

☐

28	208

☐

365	36,500

☐

1,987	19,870

☐

6	600

☐

495	4,950

☐

8,700	870

16 The model below shows $2\frac{8}{100}$ shaded.

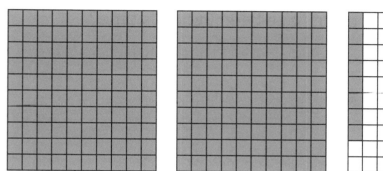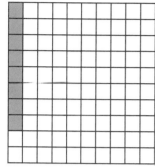

What decimal represents the shaded part of the model? Write your answer below.

_____

17 Joy started a hike at 1:50. It took Joy 2 hours and 25 minutes to finish the hike. What time did Joy finish the hike?

Ⓐ   3:35

Ⓑ   3:50

Ⓒ   4:05

Ⓓ   4:15

18 Ronald competed in a swimming race. All the students finished the race in between 42.5 seconds and 47.6 seconds. Which of the following could have been Ronald's time?

Ⓐ   41.9 seconds

Ⓑ   40.5 seconds

Ⓒ   46.8 seconds

Ⓓ   48.1 seconds

19 Which procedure can be used to find the next number in the sequence?

120, 60, 30, 15, …

Ⓐ   Subtract 15 from the previous number

Ⓑ   Add 15 to the previous number

Ⓒ   Multiply the previous number by 2

Ⓓ   Divide the previous number by 2

20 In each list below, circle the measurement that is the greatest.

List 1:   1 centimeter   1 kilometer   1 meter

List 2:   1 ounce   1 gram   1 pound

END OF PRACTICE SET

Common Core Math

Grade 4

Practice Set 10

Instructions

Read each question carefully. For each multiple-choice question, fill in the circle for the correct answer. For other types of questions, follow the directions given in the question.

You may use a ruler and a protractor to help you answer questions. You may not use a calculator on this test.

This test should take 60 minutes to complete.

1 Kevin is 1.45 meters tall. Brad is 20 centimeters taller than Kevin. What is Brad's height? Write your answer below.

_____ centimeters

2 Camilla bought 4 bags of apples. Each bag weighed $\frac{3}{8}$ pounds. What was the total weight of the apples?

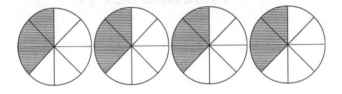

Ⓐ   3 pounds

Ⓑ $1\frac{1}{2}$ pounds

Ⓒ $1\frac{1}{8}$ pounds

Ⓓ $\frac{7}{8}$ pounds

3   Each number in Set P is related in the same way to the number beside it in Set Q.

Set P	Set Q
2	8
6	12
8	14
10	16

When given a number in Set P, what is one way to find its related number in Set Q?

Ⓐ   Multiply by 4

Ⓑ   Multiply by 2

Ⓒ   Add 6

Ⓓ   Add 8

4   In which of these does the number 8 make the equation true?

Ⓐ $48 \div \square = 6$

Ⓑ $\square \div 6 = 48$

Ⓒ $48 \times 6 = \square$

Ⓓ $\square \times 48 = 6$

5   There are 30,854 people living in Montville. Complete the missing numbers to show another way to write 30,854.

$(10{,}000 \times \boxed{}) + (100 \times \boxed{}) + (10 \times \boxed{}) + (1 \times \boxed{})$

6   What does the circled area of the diagram show?

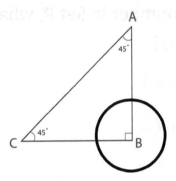

Ⓐ   A ray

Ⓑ   An angle

Ⓒ   A line segment

Ⓓ   A point

7 The line plot below shows how many goals each member of a soccer team scored in the season.

Which statement is true?

Ⓐ   Each player scored at least 1 goal.

Ⓑ   Only one player scored more than 3 goals.

Ⓒ   The same number of players scored 2 goals as scored 3 goals.

Ⓓ   More players scored 1 goal than scored no goals.

8 The population of Greenville is 609,023. What does the 9 in this number represent?

Ⓐ   Nine thousand

Ⓑ   Ninety thousand

Ⓒ   Nine hundred thousand

Ⓓ   Ninety

9   Place the numbers listed below in order from lowest to highest.

$$35.061 \quad 35.101 \quad 35.077 \quad 35.009$$

Lowest   _____

_____

_____

Highest   _____

10   Which fraction and decimal is plotted on the number line below? Circle the **two** correct answers.

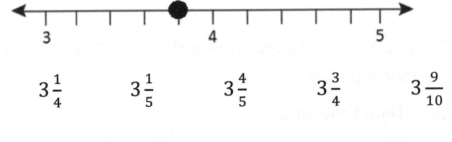

$$3\frac{1}{4} \qquad 3\frac{1}{5} \qquad 3\frac{4}{5} \qquad 3\frac{3}{4} \qquad 3\frac{9}{10}$$

3.4   3.5   3.75   3.8   3.9

11 Which is the best estimate of the angle between the hands of the clock?

Ⓐ   15°

Ⓑ   45°

Ⓒ   75°

Ⓓ   90°

12 It took Bianca 3 hours and 10 minutes to travel to her aunt's house. How long did the trip take in minutes?

Ⓐ   160 minutes

Ⓑ   180 minutes

Ⓒ   190 minutes

Ⓓ   310 minutes

13   Jed has 12 dimes, 18 nickels, and 24 pennies. He wants to divide them into as many piles as possible, but he wants the same number of dimes, nickels, and pennies in each pile.

What is the greatest number of equal piles Jed can divide the coins into? Write your answer below.

_____ piles

If Jed divides the coins into those equal piles, how many pennies will be in each pile? Write your answer below.

_____ pennies

14 In the space below, sketch and label a right angle, an acute angle, and an obtuse angle.

Right Angle

Acute Angle

Obtuse Angle

Which angle sketched had to be an exact angle measure? Explain your answer.

_____

_____

_____

_____

15 Emma grouped the numbers from 10 to 20 into prime and composite numbers. Sort the numbers from 21 to 30 into prime and composite numbers. Write each number in the correct column of the table below.

Prime		Composite	
11	13	10	12
17	19	14	15
		16	18
		20	

Explain how the prime numbers are different from composite numbers.

_____

_____

_____

_____

16 A rectangular park has a length of 80 feet and a width of 40 feet.

What is the perimeter of the park in feet? Write your answer below.

_____ feet

What is the perimeter of the park in yards? Write your answer below.

_____ yards

17 Use the model below to find the sum of $\frac{3}{10}$ and $\frac{17}{100}$. Write your answer below.

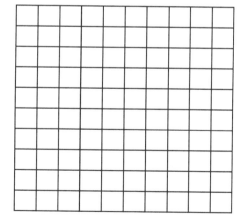

_____

18 Ben answered $\frac{70}{100}$ of the questions on a test correctly. What decimal is equivalent to $\frac{70}{100}$? Write your answer below.

_____

19 Trevor's baby sister had a nap for $1\frac{3}{4}$ hours. How many minutes did she nap for? Write your answer below.

_____ minutes

20 Circle **all** the statements that correctly describe the rhombus below.

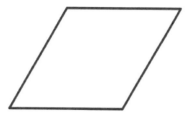

2 pairs of parallel sides

2 pairs of perpendicular sides

4 equal angles

4 right angles

4 congruent sides

Write the name of the shape that is described by **all** the statements above.

_____

END OF PRACTICE SET

ANSWER KEY

Common Core State Standards

The state of Washington has adopted the Common Core State Standards. These standards describe what students are expected to know. Student learning throughout the year is based on these standards, and all the questions on the Smarter Balanced assessments cover these standards. All the exercises and questions in this book cover the Common Core State Standards.

Assessing Skills and Knowledge

The skills listed in the Common Core State Standards are divided into five topics, or clusters. These are:

- Operations and Algebraic Thinking
- Number and Operations in Base Ten
- Number and Operations – Fractions
- Measurement and Data
- Geometry

The answer key identifies the topic for each question. Use the topics listed to identify general areas of strength and weakness. Then target revision and instruction accordingly.

The answer key also identifies the specific math skill that each question is testing. Use the skills listed to identify skills that the student is lacking. Then target revision and instruction accordingly.

Scoring Questions

This book includes questions where a task needs to be completed or a written answer is provided. The answer key gives guidance on what to look for in the answer and how to score these questions. Use the criteria listed as a guide to scoring these questions, and as a guide for giving the student advice on how to improve an answer.

Common Core Math, Practice Set 1

Question	Answer	Topic	Common Core State Standard
1	B	Number & Operations-Fractions	Understand addition and subtraction of fractions as joining and separating parts referring to the same whole.
2	1st, 3rd, and 4th	Number & Operations-Fractions	Decompose a fraction into a sum of fractions with the same denominator in more than one way, recording each decomposition by an equation.
3	D	Number & Operations-Fractions	Compare two decimals to hundredths by reasoning about their size.
4	A	Operations/Algebraic Thinking	Determine whether a given whole number in the range 1–100 is prime or composite.
5	3rd and 5th	Number & Operations-Fractions	Compare two decimals to hundredths by reasoning about their size. Record the results of comparisons with the symbols >, =, or <.
6	See Below	Number & Operations in Base Ten	Multiply two two-digit numbers, using strategies based on place value and the properties of operations. Illustrate and explain the calculation by using equations, rectangular arrays, and/or area models.
7	6, 14, 22, 30, 38	Operations/Algebraic Thinking	Generate a number or shape pattern that follows a given rule.
8	See Below	Measurement & Data	Make a line plot to display a data set of measurements in fractions of a unit (1/2, 1/4, 1/8). Solve problems involving addition and subtraction of fractions by using information presented in line plots.
9	See Below	Number & Operations-Fractions	Solve word problems involving addition and subtraction of fractions referring to the same whole and having like denominators, e.g., by using visual fraction models and equations to represent the problem.
10	See Below	Measurement & Data	Use the four operations to solve word problems involving money, including problems involving simple fractions or decimals.

Q6.
The area model should be completed with the numbers 40, 320, and 16.
Answer: 1176

Scoring Information
Give a total score out of 2.
Give a score of 1 for a correct area model.
Give a score of 1 for the correct answer.

Q8.
The line plot should be completed as shown below.

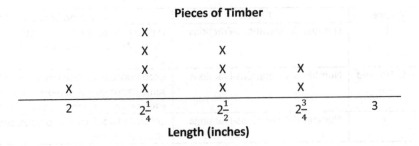

Answer: 9 inches

Scoring Information
Give a total score out of 3.
Give a score out of 2 for the line plot.
Give a score of 1 for the correct answer.

Q9.
The diagram should be shaded as shown below.

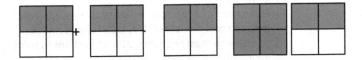

Improper fraction: $\frac{6}{4}$
Mixed number: $1\frac{1}{2}$

Scoring Information
Give a total score out of 4.
Give a score out of 2 for the shaded diagram.
Give a score of 1 for the correct improper fraction.
Give a score of 1 for the correct mixed number.

Q10.
$5.67
$6.33

Scoring Information
Give a total score out of 2.
Give a score of 1 for each correct answer.

Common Core Math, Practice Set 2

Question	Answer	Topic	Common Core State Standard
1	D	Measurement & Data	An angle that turns through 1/360 of a circle is called a "one-degree angle," and can be used to measure angles. Recognize angle measure as additive. When an angle is decomposed into non-overlapping parts, the angle measure of the whole is the sum of the angle measures of the parts.
2	1st, 2nd, 4th, and 5th	Number & Operations-Fractions	Understand addition and subtraction of fractions as joining and separating parts referring to the same whole.
3	A	Geometry	Classify two-dimensional figures based on the presence or absence of parallel or perpendicular lines, or the presence or absence of angles of a specified size.
4	B	Operations/Algebraic Thinking	Multiply or divide to solve word problems involving multiplicative comparison.
5	C	Measurement & Data	Use the four operations to solve word problems involving distances, including problems that require expressing measurements given in a larger unit in terms of a smaller unit.
6	22 tables	Number & Operations in Base Ten	Find whole-number quotients using strategies based on place value, the properties of operations, and/or the relationship between multiplication and division.
7	See Below	Measurement & Data	Recognize angle measure as additive. When an angle is decomposed into non-overlapping parts, the angle measure of the whole is the sum of the angle measures of the parts.
8	See Below	Measurement & Data	Represent and interpret data.
9	See Below	Number & Operations-Fractions	Explain why a fraction a/b is equivalent to a fraction $(n \times a)/(n \times b)$ by using visual fraction models, with attention to how the number and size of the parts differ even though the two fractions themselves are the same size. Use this principle to recognize and generate equivalent fractions.
10	See Below	Measurement & Data	Apply the area and perimeter formulas for rectangles in real world and mathematical problems.

Q7.
The straight angle should be divided into four angles of 45° each, as shown below.

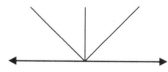

Answer: 45°
The term "acute" should be circled.

Scoring Information
Give a total score out of 3.
Give a score of 1 for dividing the straight angle correctly.
Give a score of 1 for the correct angle measure.
Give a score of 1 for circling "acute."

Q8.
The student should complete the chart as shown below.

Student Votes for Field Trip Location

Museum	✓ ✓ ✓ ✓
Cinema	✓ ✓ ✓ ✓ ✓ ✓
Zoo	✓ ✓ ✓ ✓ ✓ ✓ ✓ ✓
Town Hall	✓ ✓ ✓

✓ = 4 votes

Answer: Cinema and Town Hall

Scoring Information
Give a total score out of 3.
Give a score out of 2 for the completed picture graph.
Give a score of 1 for the correct answer.

Q9.
The student should divide each rectangle into 8 equal rectangles. The possible ways of dividing the paper are shown below.

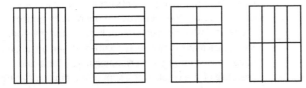

The student should explain that each piece of paper has the same area because they are all $\frac{1}{8}$ the size of the original piece of paper.

Scoring Information
Give a total score out of 4.
Give a score of 1 for each rectangle correctly divided.
Give a score out of 2 for the explanation.

Q10.
The student should add the missing dimensions 2 ft and 11 ft.
36 feet
37 tiles

Scoring Information
Give a total score out of 3.
Give a score of 0.5 for each correct dimension.
Give a score of 1 for each correct answer.

Common Core Math, Practice Set 3

Question	Answer	Topic	Common Core State Standard
1	A, C, T, W	Geometry	Identify line-symmetric figures and draw lines of symmetry.
2	B	Geometry	Draw points, lines, line segments, rays, angles (right, acute, obtuse), and perpendicular and parallel lines. Identify these in two-dimensional figures.
3	B	Measurement & Data	Use the four operations to solve word problems involving money.
4	B	Measurement & Data	Use the four operations to solve word problems involving intervals of time.
5	C, P, C, C, P, C	Operations/Algebraic Thinking	Determine whether a given whole number in the range 1–100 is prime or composite.
6	C	Number & Operations-Fractions	Decompose a fraction into a sum of fractions with the same denominator in more than one way, recording each decomposition by an equation. Justify decompositions, e.g., by using a visual fraction model.
7	2,320 2,280	Number & Operations in Base Ten	Compare two multi-digit numbers based on meanings of the digits in each place.
8	6 weeks	Operations/Algebraic Thinking	Solve multistep word problems posed with whole numbers and having whole-number answers using the four operations.
9	3 hours 50 minutes	Measurement & Data	Use the four operations to solve word problems involving intervals of time.
10	20,000 ml	Measurement & Data	Within a single system of measurement, express measurements in a larger unit in terms of a smaller unit.
11	See Below	Number & Operations in Base Ten	Compare two multi-digit numbers based on meanings of the digits in each place, using >, =, and < symbols to record the results of comparisons.
12	5,147 111	Number & Operations in Base Ten	Fluently add and subtract multi-digit whole numbers using the standard algorithm.
13	55°	Measurement & Data	Solve addition and subtraction problems to find unknown angles on a diagram in real world and mathematical problems.
14	See Below	Measurement & Data	Use the four operations to solve word problems involving distances. Apply the area and perimeter formulas for rectangles in real world and mathematical problems.
15	33, 34, 20, 80	Operations/Algebraic Thinking	Represent problems using equations with a letter standing for the unknown quantity. Assess the reasonableness of answers using mental computation and estimation strategies including rounding.
16	oval, rectangle	Operations/Algebraic Thinking	Generate a number or shape pattern that follows a given rule.
17	D	Number & Operations-Fractions	Compare two fractions with different numerators and different denominators. Justify the conclusions, e.g., by using a visual fraction model.
18	460,000 458,000	Number & Operations in Base Ten	Use place value understanding to round multi-digit whole numbers to any place.
19	A	Measurement & Data	Know relative sizes of measurement units within one system of units.
20	$0.76	Measurement & Data	Use the four operations to solve word problems involving money.

Q11.
1,461 < 1,469 < 1,487 < 1,510
Answer: 1,710

Scoring Information
Give a total score out of 3.
Give a score of 0.5 for each number correctly ordered.
Give a score of 1 for the correct answer.

Q14.
The diagram should be shaded as below.

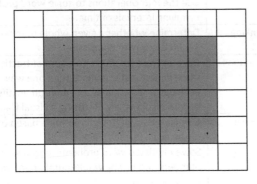

not 16/not 24

Answer: 6 square feet

Scoring Information
Give a total score out of 2.
Give a score of 1 for the correct shading.
Give a score of 1 for the correct answer.

Common Core Math, Practice Set 4

Question	Answer	Topic	Common Core State Standard
1	D	Measurement & Data	Know relative sizes of measurement units within one system of units.
2	X, M, L	Geometry	Draw points, lines, line segments, rays, angles (right, acute, obtuse), and perpendicular and parallel lines. Identify these in two-dimensional figures.
3	C	Number & Operations-Fractions	Use decimal notation for fractions with denominators 10 or 100.
4	C	Number & Operations in Base Ten	Find whole-number quotients using strategies based on place value, the properties of operations, and/or the relationship between multiplication and division.
5	Any 4 segments shaded	Number & Operations-Fractions	Explain why a fraction is equivalent to a fraction by using visual fraction models.
6	B	Operations/Algebraic Thinking	Generate and analyze patterns.
7	589 < 596 805 > 799 152 < 170	Number & Operations in Base Ten	Compare two multi-digit numbers based on meanings of the digits in each place, using >, =, and < symbols to record the results of comparisons.
8	$\frac{13}{100}$	Number & Operations-Fractions	Express a fraction with denominator 10 as an equivalent fraction with denominator 100, and use this technique to add two fractions with respective denominators 10 and 100.
9	10 pencils	Operations/Algebraic Thinking	Solve multistep word problems posed with whole numbers and having whole-number answers using the four operations, including problems in which remainders must be interpreted.
10	718 students	Number & Operations in Base Ten	Fluently add and subtract multi-digit whole numbers using the standard algorithm.
11	See Below	Number & Operations-Fractions	Decompose a fraction into a sum of fractions with the same denominator in more than one way, recording each decomposition by an equation. Justify decompositions, e.g., by using a visual fraction model.
12	4 square inches	Measurement & Data	Apply the area and perimeter formulas for rectangles in real world and mathematical problems.
13	15 nickels	Measurement & Data	Use the four operations to solve word problems involving money.
14	See Below	Geometry	Draw points, lines, line segments, rays, angles (right, acute, obtuse), and perpendicular and parallel lines. Identify these in two-dimensional figures.
15	See Below	Operations/Algebraic Thinking	Solve multistep word problems posed with whole numbers and having whole-number answers using the four operations, including problems in which remainders must be interpreted. Represent these problems using equations with a letter standing for the unknown quantity.
16	3	Operations/Algebraic Thinking	Generate and analyze patterns.
17	C	Measurement & Data	Know relative sizes of measurement units within one system of units.
18	32 and 56	Operations/Algebraic Thinking	Determine whether a given whole number in the range 1–100 is a multiple of a given one-digit number.
19	B	Number & Operations-Fractions	Understand addition and subtraction of fractions as joining and separating parts referring to the same whole.
20	See Below	Operations/Algebraic Thinking	Multiply or divide to solve word problems involving multiplicative comparison.

Q11.
The last grid of the model should have 3 of the 4 parts shaded.

Answer: $\frac{3}{4}$

The explanation should refer to the diagram showing that 3 of the 4 parts of the whole are shaded.

Scoring Information
Give a total score out of 3.
Give a score of 1 for the correct shading.
Give a score of 1 for the correct answer.
Give a score out of 1 for the explanation.

Q14.
The two smallest angles should be circled.
The explanation should refer to how you can tell that the angles are less than a right angle.

Scoring Information
Give a total score out of 3.
Give a score of 1 for each correct angle circled.
Give a score out of 1 for the explanation.

Q15.
$c = 2d + 4$
Answer: $16

Scoring Information
Give a total score out of 3.
Give a score of 1 for the correct equation.
Give a score of 1 for the correct answer.
Give a score of 1 for using the correct value of $d = 6$.

Q20.
35 hours
45 hours
40 hours
$270

Scoring Information
Give a total score out of 4.
Give a score of 1 for each correct answer.

Common Core Math, Practice Set 5

Question	Answer	Topic	Common Core State Standard
1	26 cm 30 cm^2	Measurement & Data	Apply the area and perimeter formulas for rectangles in real world and mathematical problems.
2	4, 9	Operations/Algebraic Thinking	Recognize that a whole number is a multiple of each of its factors.
3	Fruit juice, Quiche	Measurement & Data	Use the four operations to solve word problems involving money.
4	B	Operations/Algebraic Thinking	Solve multistep word problems posed with whole numbers and having whole-number answers using the four operations.
5	B	Operations/Algebraic Thinking	Assess the reasonableness of answers using mental computation and estimation strategies including rounding.
6	960 beads	Number & Operations in Base Ten	Multiply a whole number of up to four digits by a one-digit whole number using strategies based on place value and the properties of operations.
7	A	Number & Operations-Fractions	Apply and extend previous understandings of multiplication to multiply a fraction by a whole number.
8	165°	Measurement & Data	Measure angles in whole-number degrees using a protractor.
9	A	Number & Operations in Base Ten	Find whole-number quotients and remainders with up to four-digit dividends and one-digit divisors.
10	D	Operations/Algebraic Thinking	Find all factor pairs for a whole number in the range 1–100.
11	12, 14, 30, 54, 66	Operations/Algebraic Thinking	Determine whether a given whole number in the range 1–100 is a multiple of a given one-digit number.
12	255,000 grams	Measurement & Data	Within a single system of measurement, express measurements in a larger unit in terms of a smaller unit.
13	C	Number & Operations-Fractions	Use decimal notation for fractions with denominators 10 or 100.
14	6	Measurement & Data	Record measurement equivalents in a two-column table.
15	C	Geometry	Draw and identify right, acute, and obtuse angles.
16	D	Measurement & Data	Know relative sizes of measurement units within one system of units.
17	A	Number & Operations in Base Ten	Read and write multi-digit whole numbers using base-ten numerals, number names, and expanded form.
18	A	Operations/Algebraic Thinking	Generate and analyze patterns.
19	3rd and 6th	Measurement & Data	Use the four operations to solve word problems involving money.
20	6	Number & Operations in Base Ten	Find whole-number quotients using strategies based on place value, the properties of operations, and/or the relationship between multiplication and division.

Common Core Math, Practice Set 6

Question	Answer	Topic	Common Core State Standard
1	D	Measurement & Data	Within a single system of measurement, express measurements in a larger unit in terms of a smaller unit.
2	D	Operations/Algebraic Thinking	Assess the reasonableness of answers using mental computation and estimation strategies including rounding.
3	C	Number & Operations in Base Ten	Recognize that in a multi-digit whole number, a digit in one place represents ten times what it represents in the place to its right.
4	1st, 3rd, and 4th	Geometry	Identify line-symmetric figures and draw lines of symmetry.
5	July June $9.25	Number & Operations-Fractions	Compare two decimals to hundredths by reasoning about their size.
6	57, 247, 121, 93	Operations/Algebraic Thinking	Determine whether a given whole number in the range 1–100 is prime or composite.
7	4th and 5th	Number & Operations-Fractions	Compare two fractions with different numerators and different denominators.
8	C	Operations/Algebraic Thinking	Generate and analyze patterns.
9	64 square inches	Measurement & Data	Apply the area and perimeter formulas for rectangles in real world and mathematical problems.
10	Q and T R and S	Geometry	Identify perpendicular and parallel lines in two-dimensional figures.
11	B	Measurement & Data	Know relative sizes of measurement units within one system of units.
12	D	Number & Operations in Base Ten	Read and write multi-digit whole numbers using base-ten numerals, number names, and expanded form.
13	2.4	Number & Operations-Fractions	Use decimal notation for fractions with denominators 10 or 100.
14	A	Number & Operations in Base Ten	Read and write multi-digit whole numbers using base-ten numerals, number names, and expanded form.
15	C	Measurement & Data	Solve addition and subtraction problems to find unknown angles on a diagram.
16	77, 81, 91	Operations/Algebraic Thinking	Determine whether a given whole number in the range 1–100 is prime or composite.
17	83,500 83,460	Number & Operations in Base Ten	Use place value understanding to round multi-digit whole numbers to any place.
18	60 and 6,000 6 and 600	Number & Operations in Base Ten	Recognize that in a multi-digit whole number, a digit in one place represents ten times what it represents in the place to its right.
19	D	Measurement & Data	Measure angles in whole-number degrees using a protractor.
20	$1.36 2 quarters and a nickel $0.81	Measurement & Data	Use the four operations to solve word problems involving money.

Common Core Math, Practice Set 7

Question	Answer	Topic	Common Core State Standard
1	D	Geometry	Identify perpendicular and parallel lines in two-dimensional figures.
2	C	Number & Operations-Fractions	Recognize and generate equivalent fractions.
3	B	Number & Operations-Fractions	Compare two decimals to hundredths by reasoning about their size.
4	B	Number & Operations-Fractions	Solve word problems involving multiplication of a fraction by a whole number.
5	D	Operations/Algebraic Thinking	Assess the reasonableness of answers using mental computation and estimation strategies including rounding.
6	24	Operations/Algebraic Thinking	Solve multistep word problems posed with whole numbers and having whole-number answers using the four operations.
7	D	Number & Operations in Base Ten	Fluently add and subtract multi-digit whole numbers using the standard algorithm.
8	72, 36, 280, 333	Number & Operations in Base Ten	Multiply a whole number of up to four digits by a one-digit whole number.
9	A	Operations/Algebraic Thinking	Solve multistep word problems posed with whole numbers and having whole-number answers using the four operations.
10	A	Operations/Algebraic Thinking	Represent problems using equations with a letter standing for the unknown quantity.
11	C	Number & Operations in Base Ten	Recognize that in a multi-digit whole number, a digit in one place represents ten times what it represents in the place to its right.
12	B	Geometry	Identify line-symmetric figures and draw lines of symmetry.
13	See Below	Number & Operations-Fractions	Understand decimal notation for fractions, and compare decimal fractions.
14	See Below	Number & Operations-Fractions	Build fractions from unit fractions by applying and extending previous understandings of operations on whole numbers.
15	See Below	Operations/Algebraic Thinking	Generate a number or shape pattern that follows a given rule. Identify apparent features of the pattern that were not explicit in the rule itself.
16	See Below	Geometry	Recognize a line of symmetry for a two-dimensional figure as a line across the figure such that the figure can be folded along the line into matching parts.
17	See Below	Number & Operations in Base Ten	Read and write multi-digit whole numbers using base-ten numerals, number names, and expanded form.
18	156 students	Number & Operations in Base Ten	Multiply a whole number of up to four digits by a one-digit whole number using strategies based on place value and the properties of operations.
19	2,400 square feet	Measurement & Data	Apply the area and perimeter formulas for rectangles in real world and mathematical problems.
20	See Below	Geometry	Classify two-dimensional figures based on the presence or absence of parallel or perpendicular lines, or the presence or absence of angles of a specified size.

Q13.
The number 1.75 should be plotted on the number line.
Answer: $1\frac{3}{4}$ or $1\frac{75}{100}$

Scoring Information
Give a total score out of 2.
Give a score of 1 for the number correctly plotted.
Give a score of 1 for the correct answer.

Q14.
The model should be shaded as shown below.

Answer: $\frac{17}{10}$

Scoring Information
Give a total score out of 2.
Give a score of 1 for the correct shading.
Give a score of 1 for the correct answer.

Q15.
Answer: 41
The student should explain that each number in the pattern is 6 more than the one before it, and that the next number is found by adding 6 to the last number, 35.
The student should identify that every number in the pattern will be odd. The explanation should show an understanding that every step involves adding an even number to an odd number.

Scoring Information
Give a total score out of 4.
Give a score of 1 for the correct answer.
Give a score out of 1 for the explanation.
Give a score of 1 for correctly identifying that every number will be odd.
Give a score out of 1 for the explanation.

Q16.
The isosceles triangle in the center should be identified as the shape that has a line of symmetry. A line of symmetry should be drawn on the triangle, as shown below.

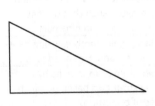 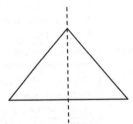 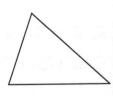

The student may describe how the two halves are the same size and shape or how the two halves can be folded onto each other.

Scoring Information
Give a total score out of 4.
Give a score of 1 for the correct shape identified.
Give a score of 1 for the line of symmetry drawn correctly.
Give a score out of 2 for the explanation.

Q17.

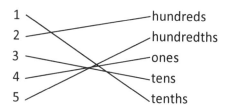

$2 \times 100 + 3 \times 10 + 4 \times 1 + 1 \times \frac{1}{10} + 5 \times \frac{1}{100}$

Scoring Information
Give a total score out of 2.
Give a score of 1 for identifying place values correctly.
Give a score of 1 for writing the number in expanded form correctly.

Q20.
The column for 1 or more right angles should list A, C, and D.
The column for 1 or more pairs of parallel sides should list A, D, E, and F.
The column for 1 or more pairs of perpendicular sides should list A, C, and D.

Scoring Information
Give a total score out of 3.
Give a score of 1 for each column correctly completed.

Common Core Math, Practice Set 8

Question	Answer	Topic	Common Core State Standard
1	165 minutes	Measurement & Data	Use the four operations to solve word problems involving intervals of time.
2	B	Operations/Algebraic Thinking	Solve multistep word problems posed with whole numbers and having whole-number answers using the four operations, including problems in which remainders must be interpreted.
3	D	Operations/Algebraic Thinking	Find all factor pairs for a whole number in the range 1–100. / Determine whether a given whole number in the range 1–100 is prime or composite.
4	$6 \times t = 42$	Operations/Algebraic Thinking	Represent problems using equations with a letter standing for the unknown quantity.
5	C	Number & Operations-Fractions	Understand addition and subtraction of fractions as joining and separating parts referring to the same whole.
6	5	Operations/Algebraic Thinking	Find all factor pairs for a whole number in the range 1–100.
7	B	Operations/Algebraic Thinking	Assess the reasonableness of answers using mental computation and estimation strategies including rounding.
8	A	Operations/Algebraic Thinking	Solve multistep word problems posed with whole numbers and having whole-number answers using the four operations.
9	C	Measurement & Data	Use the four operations to solve word problems involving money.
10	C	Measurement & Data	Know relative sizes of measurement units within one system of units.
11	2nd, 5th, 6th	Operations/Algebraic Thinking	Find all factor pairs for a whole number in the range 1–100. / Determine whether a given whole number in the range 1–100 is prime or composite.
12	÷ 3	Operations/Algebraic Thinking	Generate and analyze patterns.
13	D	Number & Operations in Base Ten	Recognize that in a multi-digit whole number, a digit in one place represents ten times what it represents in the place to its right.
14	7 people	Measurement & Data	Solve problems by using information presented in line plots.
15	Any 2 segments shaded	Number & Operations-Fractions	Understand, recognize, and generate equivalent fractions using visual fraction models, with attention to how the number and size of the parts differ even though the two fractions themselves are the same size.
16	0.14	Number & Operations-Fractions	Use decimal notation for fractions with denominators 10 or 100.
17	A	Number & Operations-Fractions	Record the results of comparisons with symbols >, =, or <, and justify the conclusions, e.g., by using a visual fraction model.
18	C	Operations/Algebraic Thinking	Assess the reasonableness of answers using mental computation and estimation strategies including rounding.
19	24 pints 48 cups	Measurement & Data	Within a single system of measurement, express measurements in a larger unit in terms of a smaller unit.
20	B	Measurement & Data	Solve addition and subtraction problems to find unknown angles on a diagram in real world and mathematical problems.

Common Core Math, Practice Set 9

Question	Answer	Topic	Common Core State Standard
1	A	Operations/Algebraic Thinking	Generate and analyze patterns.
2	A	Number & Operations-Fractions	Use decimal notation for fractions with denominators 10 or 100.
3	C	Geometry	Identify perpendicular and parallel lines in two-dimensional figures.
4	Vertical line at center of pentagon, horizontal line at center of trapezoid	Geometry	Identify line-symmetric figures and draw lines of symmetry.
5	D	Operations/Algebraic Thinking	Represent verbal statements of multiplicative comparisons as multiplication equations.
6	A	Geometry	Recognize right triangles as a category, and identify right triangles.
7	B	Number & Operations-Fractions	Decompose a fraction into a sum of fractions with the same denominator in more than one way, recording each decomposition by an equation.
8	Ford, Toyota, Saturn, Honda	Number & Operations in Base Ten	Compare two multi-digit numbers based on meanings of the digits in each place.
9	4	Number & Operations in Base Ten	Find whole-number quotients using strategies based on place value, the properties of operations, and/or the relationship between multiplication and division.
10	D	Measurement & Data	Know relative sizes of measurement units within one system of units.
11	3 of 5 segments shaded 60 of 100 segments shaded $\frac{3}{5}$ and $\frac{60}{100}$	Number & Operations-Fractions	Understand, recognize, and generate equivalent fractions using visual fraction models, with attention to how the number and size of the parts differ even though the two fractions themselves are the same size.
12	15	Operations/Algebraic Thinking	Generate and analyze patterns.
13	D	Number & Operations in Base Ten	Read and write multi-digit whole numbers using base-ten numerals, number names, and expanded form.
14	C	Measurement & Data	Represent measurement quantities using diagrams such as number line diagrams that feature a measurement scale.
15	3rd and 5th	Number & Operations in Base Ten	Recognize that in a multi-digit whole number, a digit in one place represents ten times what it represents in the place to its right.
16	2.08	Number & Operations-Fractions	Use decimal notation for fractions with denominators 10 or 100.
17	D	Measurement & Data	Use the four operations to solve word problems involving time.
18	C	Number & Operations-Fractions	Compare two decimals to hundredths by reasoning about their size.
19	D	Operations/Algebraic Thinking	Generate and analyze patterns.
20	1 kilometer 1 pound	Measurement & Data	Know relative sizes of measurement units within one system of units.

Common Core Math, Practice Set 10

Question	Answer	Topic	Common Core State Standard
1	165 centimeters	Measurement & Data	Use the four operations to solve word problems involving distances, including problems involving simple fractions or decimals.
2	B	Number & Operations-Fractions	Solve word problems involving multiplication of a fraction by a whole number.
3	C	Operations/Algebraic Thinking	Generate and analyze patterns.
4	A	Number & Operations in Base Ten	Find whole-number quotients using strategies based on place value, the properties of operations, and/or the relationship between multiplication and division.
5	3, 8, 5, 4	Number & Operations in Base Ten	Read and write multi-digit whole numbers using base-ten numerals, number names, and expanded form.
6	B	Measurement & Data	Recognize angles as geometric shapes that are formed wherever two rays share a common endpoint.
7	B	Measurement & Data	Solve problems by using information presented in line plots.
8	A	Number & Operations in Base Ten	Recognize that in a multi-digit whole number, a digit in one place represents ten times what it represents in the place to its right.
9	35.009 35.061 35.077 35.101	Number & Operations-Fractions	Compare two decimals to hundredths by reasoning about their size.
10	$3\frac{4}{5}$, 3.8	Number & Operations-Fractions	Use decimal notation for fractions with denominators 10 or 100.
11	B	Measurement & Data	Understand concepts of angle measurement, including that an angle is measured with reference to a circle with its center at the common endpoint of the rays, and that an angle that turns through 1/360 of a circle is called a "one-degree angle," and can be used to measure angles.
12	C	Measurement & Data	Within a single system of measurement, express measurements in a larger unit in terms of a smaller unit.
13	6 piles 4 pennies	Operations/Algebraic Thinking	Multiply or divide to solve word problems involving multiplicative comparison.
14	See Below	Measurement & Data	Sketch angles of specified measure.
15	See Below	Operations/Algebraic Thinking	Determine whether a given whole number in the range 1–100 is prime or composite.
16	240 feet 80 yards	Measurement & Data	Apply the area and perimeter formulas for rectangles in real world and mathematical problems.
17	$\frac{47}{100}$	Number & Operations-Fractions	Express a fraction with denominator 10 as an equivalent fraction with denominator 100, and use this technique to add two fractions with respective denominators 10 and 100.
18	0.7	Number & Operations-Fractions	Use decimal notation for fractions with denominators 10 or 100.

19	105 minutes	Measurement & Data	Use the four operations to solve word problems involving intervals of time, including problems involving simple fractions or decimals, and problems that require expressing measurements given in a larger unit in terms of a smaller unit.
20	See Below	Geometry	Classify two-dimensional figures based on the presence or absence of parallel or perpendicular lines, or the presence or absence of angles of a specified size.

Q14.
The student should sketch a right angle equal to 90°, an acute angle of less than 90°, and an obtuse angle greater than 90°. The explanation should show an understanding that the right angle must be 90°, while the other two angles do not have to be an exact measure.

Scoring Information
Give a total score out of 4.
Give a score of 0.5 for each angle correctly sketched.
Give a score of 0.5 for identifying that the right angle had to be exact.
Give a score out of 2 for the explanation.

Q15.
Prime: 23, 29
Composite: 21, 22, 24, 25, 26, 27, 28, 30
The student should explain that prime numbers can only be divided by themselves and 1, while composite numbers can be divided by at least one other number.

Scoring Information
Give a total score out of 4.
Give a score out of 2 for sorting the numbers correctly.
Give a score out of 2 for the explanation.

Q20.
The statements "2 pairs of parallel sides" and "4 congruent sides" should be circled.
square

Scoring Information
Give a total score out of 3.
Give a score of 1 for each correct statement circled. Take off 1 point if additional statements are circled.
Give a score of 1 for the correct answer of square.

Made in United States
Troutdale, OR
04/29/2025

30997428R00077